Blog Writing

The Content Creation Blueprint

(How to Master Content Creation to Propel Your Blog On to the Next Level and Make Even More Serious Money Online)

Anthony James

© Copyright 2018 by Anthony James

All rights reserved.

The following eBook is reproduced below with the goal of providing information that is as accurate and reliable as possible. Regardless, purchasing this eBook can be seen as consent to the fact that both the publisher and the author of this book are in no way experts on the topics discussed within and that any recommendations or suggestions that are made herein are for entertainment purposes only. Professionals should be consulted as needed prior to undertaking any of the action endorsed herein.

This declaration is deemed fair and valid by both the American Bar Association and the Committee of Publishers Association and is legally binding throughout the United States.

Furthermore, the transmission, duplication or reproduction of any of the following work, including specific information, will be considered an illegal act irrespective of if it is done electronically or in print. This extends to creating a secondary or tertiary copy of the work or a recorded copy and is only allowed with express written consent from the Publisher. All additional right reserved.

The information in the following pages is broadly considered to be a truthful and accurate account of facts and as such any inattention, use or misuse of the information in question by the reader will render any resulting actions solely under their purview. There are no scenarios in which the publisher or the original author of this work can be in any fashion deemed liable for any hardship or damages that may befall them after undertaking information described herein.

Additionally, the information in the following pages is intended only for informational purposes and should thus be thought of as universal. As befitting its nature, it is presented without assurance regarding its prolonged validity or interim quality. Trademarks that are mentioned are done without written consent and can in no way be considered an endorsement from the trademark holder.

Table of Contents

Introduction 4

Chapter One 9

Content Planning: Understanding Why You Need to Create Content Consistently? 9

Chapter Two 23

Power-Packed Headline Creation Strategies 23

Chapter Three 36

Secrets for Curating and Rewriting Great Content ... 36

Chapter Four: 14 Types of Content That Can Sky-Rocket Your Blog Traffic 63

Chapter Five: 10 Content Marketing Tips to Take Your Blog into the Next League 81

Conclusion 89

Introduction

Assume you walk into a store to buy a bottle of perfume. The salesperson greets you warmly and goes on to ask you the fragrance you are looking for. He/she chats with you about your typical usage, preferences, and habits. Do you need a more flirty, casual fragrance or a more formal, long-wearing one? Do you keep reusing it often throughout the day or is a one-time application good enough to last throughout the day? The salesperson also informs you about the latest products, how smell affects your mood and other interesting and fascinating details. You strike up a conversation, and before you know, you have bought a ton of stuff from them.

Compare this with walking into a shop and being pitched the most expensive fragrances available without trying to understand what you are looking for or offering you any information (i.e., value) about your purchases. There's no attempt to strike a dialogue or offer value. The person is simply interested in selling rather than helping you buy.

Little wonder then, that you will not buy as much in the second scenario unless you know exactly what you want, and you will be scooting out once you have bought your items without establishing any buyer relationship with the salesperson.

Now think of your blog as the store and your audience as your buyers. Can you simply pitch your business opportunity to internet users without establishing a connection of trust with them? Can you create a loyal community of readers without establishing your authority and credibility?

Hear this loud and clear: people are tired of being spammed and being exposed to a truckload of promotional crap every day. They seek value. Real, solid and relevant value. They are looking for material that is valuable to them and can be quickly applied in their life to solve their most pressing concerns or make things easier for them.

If you are not focusing on a clear content strategy or not sharing real value, you are leaving a ton of money on the table for your competitors. Real, targeted and interested customer leads can be generated only when people are convinced that you can offer them real value.

While spamming social media pages may seem like a quick fix solution to generate some speedy leads, it is a dead end for businesses that will be around for a long time. If you are looking to build a solid, stable and consistent source of long-term income, content is the life blood of your business. The most profitable and leveraged way to get customers to buy from you is to offer them solid value.

Great content helps in building your brand. It also helps in establishing your authority in the given domain. (Who doesn't prefer buying from an expert who knows everything about a particular niche?) A strong content strategy creates sufficient interest in and awareness of your product. Integrating content into the sales process makes it all the more efficient than simply pushing your product on the customer. It makes your brand comes across as likable, relatable, identifiable and human. No one likes to be sold to by bots. Buyers love to buy from real humans with whom they can establish connections. And what better way to establish a dialogue with people than giving them valuable and powerful content that has the potential to impact their lives?

A strong, clear and consistent content strategy helps you build a following of loyal customers who make repeat purchases from you. You do not just make new customers; you also retain the existing ones by offering them sheer value.

Let's dive head first into this fascinating world of content marketing, and begin to master content creation to put your blog on the highway to success.

Chapter One

Content Planning: Understanding Why You Need to Create Content Consistently?

You might be wondering why must you have a clear, coherent and long-term content plan.

Don't misunderstand. Having a content plan or strategy does not mean mapping out every piece of content you will post for the coming year. It simply means that you establish a set of parameters and guidelines for content creation to accomplish specific, higher objectives as you progress.

The goals can be things such as increasing your followers, converting followers into buyers or turning buyers into loyal, repeat customers.

Here are the top reasons why you should have a clear content plan/strategy and consistent content in place if you are serious about turning your blog into a money making machine.

1. Long Term Gains

Think about it. Would you rather invest in one-time scattered promotional or long-term content that requires work once and then can be leveraged multiple times? You create a well-researched, insightful and detailed blog post once and your audience will lap it up for several years to come, without it requiring any additional work from you.

That is the beauty of earning passive income online. You work once and reap its benefits almost forever. Having a blog populated with valuable content gives you the opportunity to earn revenue from it steadily and consistently.

2. Streamlined Efforts

Working on a blog without a clear content plan is like driving to an unknown destination without a map (or Google Maps for millennials). Plans streamline your content and give your blog a sense of direction. Production becomes easier when you have planned ahead about what goes into the blog.

Content can be anything from a holiday season infographic, a timely review of a new product or a detailed, analytical piece created to establish your authority and drive sales during a particular season. Long term content planning gives a clear focus on creating timely content and powerful content ideas to fulfill business goals.

3. Brings Steadiness and Consistency

Have you ever invested in the stock market? You do not always get immediate returns unless you are really lucky and even then that is more likely be an exception than rule.

You cannot build a successful blog simply by creating a couple of viral posts, and hoping they will work wonders for you. A solid content strategy ensures you have a regular and steady flow of content over a period of time, some of which can work brilliantly for you.

Driving traffic to your blog is all about the law of averages at the end of the day. No one really knows what will become a viral sensation that drives thousands of visitors to your blog. You need to have a lot of quality content on your blog if you wish to make money from it because you do not know what posts will work and what will not. A steady flow of content ensures you are not investing all your precious resources into a few posts that you hope will go viral.

For instance, if you have a hundred posts on your blog, even if only 25 to 30 perform exceptionally well, you may well be laughing your way to the bank. It is all a game of numbers so the higher the number of great quality posts you put on your blog, the higher your chances will be of making consistent profits from it.

4. Time Saving

Imagine a scenario where you are managing multiple blogs. Can you really invest time on each of them daily or would you rather plan and keep their content ready in advance to simply post at a convenient time each day? Also, imagine waking up each day and not knowing what to write or post for the day.

Planning your content strategy saves times and allows you to cover days when you may be busier than usual. It is easier to multitask when you have everything ready in advance. You do not waste time trying to figure out what to do next. You invest some time, in the beginning, to put a plan in place and implement it on a weekly or daily basis to fulfill your blogging goals.

5. Boosted Lead Conversions

A well-planned content strategy means making consistent efforts to get your readers to spend greater time on your blog, thus engaging them to boost your conversion rate. Useful content builds trust and sets the stage for people to buy from you. The results may not be immediate, but they can be surprisingly large! Think of it as harvesting a crop.

When you sow the seeds on your farm land, the returns or results are not immediate. You keep watering the seeds, use good quality fertilizers and undertake periodic weeding to reap a rich harvest. The end result? You harvest a flourishing batch of crops after a period of time.

Blogging is really no different. You sow the seeds of great content on your blogging farmland. You water it periodically by updating the content, weed out the spam, and use proven software tools to help you reap rich rewards from loyal, engaged readers who trust you. Credibility, authority, and expertise boost conversions and help you accomplish the desired results. The results may not be instant, but over a period of time you could end up reaping rich rewards from your consistent efforts.

Remember the salesperson example at the beginning of the book? The salesperson who builds a rapport with his/her customer has higher chances of making the sale over someone who does not care to build a rapport.

Readers are likelier to buy from you when you help them buy and don't merely try to sell.

6. Higher Search Engine Rank

Don't try to kid yourself by saying you are not writing for Google or you do not care about search engines. The fact is, however strong your promotion/marketing/advertising strategy is, everyone can do with a little organic promotion boost. Even though search engines have highly complicated algorithms that are tough to crack, it is fairly safe to say that content is a vital component of it.

Using the right keywords, creating detailed and well-researched content relevant to those keywords, and using multiple presentation formats (videos, photographs, infographics) boost your chances of ranking high on search engines.

Well-optimized blogs that have the right keywords and backlinks are favorably viewed by the big G and other search engines. It is no secret that Google loves long, detailed, visual-rich posts that pack in plenty of informational value for the reader.

They want to improve their user experience and hence rank posts that offer users detailed and relevant information in an easily digestible format.

Content planning equips you with the ability to create a steady flow of content for boosting your SEO efforts. The more content you create, the higher your chances will be of being found on search engines by your target market.

7. Higher Traffic

More keywords and focused blog posts mean reaching a higher number of interested readers, who will be keen to know more about your products or services. Imagine having a single post that's performing/ranking well on search engines. You will draw readers who are interested in reading that particular post.

Now, imagine a few hundred posts performing well on search engines. Can you image your organic reach and the number of people you will be drawing to your blog? Also, more posts mean greater sharing on social media, which can be a goldmine for targeted customers. If you have multiple thoughtfully written and interesting posts going viral, your blog will draw higher traffic.

People invariably share content that makes them look smart and well-informed among their social circle. If you take the trouble to put together a content plan about creating awesome content you are literally saying to people, "come share this great piece of content with your friends to show them how well-read and smart you are." This leads to more sharing, a greater buzz about your blog, and eventually higher traffic. Not bad for a little streamlined planning!

8. Creates a Desirable Brand

A clear, creative and strong content strategy helps create awareness about your brand. It helps your audience identify with the brand and connect with them at a subconscious level to make your brand more desirable. It is easier to get people to buy from you when they can connect with your brand values.

Content creation helps you create a more identifiable and likable brand that people can relate to. Say for instance you have a blog dedicated to helping people who are going through a painful marriage or relationship. You make money by promoting other people's eBooks (affiliate marketing) on saving marriages or preparing for a divorce.

When you create posts that resonate with people (how to help your children cope with a separation or how to help children heal after breaking away from an abusive relationship) and offer them solutions, they can relate to your brand.

When people identify and relate to your brand, it is easier for them to forge connections and buy from you. A strong content strategy demonstrates that you know enough about a subject to make expert, life-improving recommendations to them. Great content invariably creates a desirable and irresistible brand that people love to follow.

Engaged followers/readers make for more willing buyers. They are more open to recommendations and solutions originating from an authoritative source. In an era where businesses mushroom by the hour, great content prevents people from forgetting your brand. Engaged users are some of the best evangelists for your brand. They help to endorse your brand without a need for you to aggressively promote it in coming years.

When people read anything on your blog, they are unknowingly forming an impression about your brand values. If they come across content that is informative, insightful and enlightening, they are likely to think positively about your brand. If they see your content consistently shared on social media, your brand appears more established and trustworthy in the industry.

9. Establishes Expertise

Consistently writing high-quality posts boosts the perceived authority, expertise and credibility of your blog. When other blogs link to your well-written posts, your blog domain authority increases. It acts as a sort of validation for your expertise among your target audience.

Higher domain authority again translates into boosted search engine rankings, which makes your blog content even more visible. Great quality content created through smart content planning strategies increases your blog's organic visibility.

Audience recognition and connections are an important strategy for any business, and blogging is no exception. If you use individuals to create and share content, people could develop a closer association or more intimate relationship with them, and eventually your brand. You will become their go-to place for any information related to the topic, thus strengthening their loyalty.

Basics of Content Planning

1. Set content goals. What is the main objective of your content strategy? Who are the end users of the content? What do you want them to gain from the content? What should be covered in the content? The objectives should be clearly communicated to your team of writers and designers so the content and design are consistent.

2. Create Timelines. Sticking to a schedule is extremely important when it comes to content creation. Your chances of profiting from your posts increase when you post consistently on schedule. It can be a blog post a day, or two to three posts spread throughout the week. However you do it, posting regularly is a must if you want to build a steady income from it.

3. Document a strategy. Create a sheet where

everyone can reference the team's content creation strategy to eliminate miscommunication. Put together an editorial calendar that lists the blog topic, the name of the author and the date the post is scheduled to be published.

4. Ensure deadlines are met. Equip your team of writers or designers with the available resources to turn around quick and high-quality work that is on schedule. Defaulting on deadlines means your content does not go up at the scheduled, which can result in a loss of engagement and revenue.

Chapter Two

Power-Packed Headline Creation Strategies

Now that we know why creating content consistently is so important, and the basics of content planning, it's time to notch up the learning a bit. Let's learn more about creating awesome, mind-blowing content that your readers just cannot get enough of. What is it that distinguishes average content from fabulous pieces that are shared all over the internet? Here are some expert content creation tips.

Secret Formula for Crafting Sticky Blog Headlines

(There I had your attention, didn't I?)

"On the average, five times as many people read the headline as read the body copy. When you have written your headline, you have spent eighty cents out of your dollar."
— David Ogilvy

The headline is really the backbone of your content. Of course, you cannot simply create a brilliant headline to peddle lousy content. However, an attention-grabbing, eye-catching and interesting headline can give huge momentum to your content piece.

The trouble most bloggers or writers have is that they spend hours writing the perfect blog copy and devote little time to the headline. This means the post fails to grab their reader's attention. And unfortunately, this means the perfectly written blog copy does not get read.

Did you know that nearly 8 out of 10 people read just a headline, while only 2 out of 10 take time to read the entire post? A great headline can increase the number of visitors on your blog.

It will boost the chances of your content being read and shared by readers.

So what are some of the best tips for writing sticky headlines?

1. **Appeal to people's most primal emotions**

Emotions such as fear, joy, unhappiness, humor, etc. Make your headlines a mix of emotion and logic. Reinforce a problem and pitch your post as a solution for that problem.

Headlines should first grab people's attention by appealing to a strong emotion, and then compel them to read it by offering a solution or strong value proposition. For instance:

Struggling to Come Up with the Perfect Blog Headline? Here Are Some Fool-Proof Tips!

Worried About Your Student Loans? Here's Our Secret Formula for Leading a Debt Free Life!

Begin with a rough, working title. You most likely will not have your 'wow' headline dawn upon you in a Eureka moment (though as you practice, this will happen more often).

A working title gives a clear angle to a broad topic. It gives a specific guideline tone to the post while making it more targeted. For instance, raising intelligent kids can be a fairly broad topic, which people may have seen on a hundred other blogs about parenting.

However, you can make it super specific by using a headline such as "10 Foods That Can Strengthen Your Child's Memory" or "Quick Mind Exercises to Sharpen Your Kid's Brain." Contrast these headlines with "How to Raise Intelligent Kids?" The first headlines are more specific and attention grabbing. They are clear about what readers can expect in the post.

The broad headline does not pique your curiosity because it seems vague and does not tell you precisely what aspect of raising intelligent children is being covered in the post.

Did you know that in an attention starved world where people are constantly bombarded with information, they decide whether they want to spend time reading or not reading something within seconds?

Start with a specific working title (keep it narrow), and keep working on it as you create your post copy. Once you have a headline to guide your post, you can keep improving it until you are ready to publish.

2. Stay Factual and Accurate.

Set the right expectations while writing headlines for your blogs. A headline like, "20 Companies Who Are Slaying It with Twitter So Freaking Amazingly They Do Not Use Other Advertising Channels" is slightly pretentious and quite over the top. Do not make bombastic, exaggerated claims for some quick page views.

This is nothing but a form of click bait, where you create misleading, false or inaccurate headlines just to get people to click on a link. It can end up hurting the credibility and authenticity of your blog heavily. If you are in it for the long haul, avoid inaccurate headlines like the plague.

3. Use the power of numbers.

If you head to your nearest grocery store and scan through a magazine or tabloid headlines, you will notice how they effectively use numbers to grab the reader's attention. Strange as it may seem, obscure numbers are believed to grab the reader's attention. So now you know, why those "37 Perfect Destinations for A Summer Wedding" or "11 Easy and Healthy Drinks to Beat Your Summer Blues" are so popular.

4. Tap into people's hot buttons by using "trigger" words.

There is always a more effective and impactful way to convey an idea. Include actionable verbs and interesting adjectives that cause people to read the post.

So, you can have a headline like, "Top 10 Things to Do When You Are Feeling Depressed."

Or you can convey the same idea with, "10 Incredible Ways to Beat Depression." We just repackaged the headline into something more enticing and attractive by including an actionable verb and compelling adjective.

Headlines are all about saying a lot with very few words. Try to communicate the essence of your post while still using as few words as possible to retain its impact.

Use words such as effortless, genuine, honest, free, fun, essential, strange, incredible, absolute, delighted, proven, secrets, tricks, ideas and other similar terms to gain people's attention and trust.

5. Make it Bold.

Promise your reader something insanely valuable and fulfill that promise. It can be anything such as learning new skills, persuading the reader to do something they have never done before or unlocking a mystery. Offer the reader a bold and clear value proposition.

What you are doing is daring the reader to read the post. Be bold without overpromising or sounding preposterous. Be seductive (not in the literal sense, of course) and dangerous. And then deliver.

6. Make it sexy aye!

Have some fun and make your title eye popping and sexy. Add a dash of zing to it by understanding your buyer's primary persona. Use words and phrases that resonate with the reader.

Playing with alliteration is a good idea for drafting sexy sounding headlines. Phrases like "Secret Strategies" and "Fool-Proof Formula" have a subtle yet powerful impact.

Strong language also makes for sexy headlines, even if you use negative language to create a bit of a stir, such as "Things -------- Hate." However, make sure you are using the negative technique in moderation. If you try to make everything bold instead of keeping a few things bold, the gravity of the boldness is lost.

7. Keep your headlines short.

There is no standard size for a headline of course, but it should be succinct and crisp enough to keep your reader hooked. Do not make it long winded and verbose. Keep it brief, pithy and interesting. If you make your blog title more than 70 characters, it will be slashed by search engines, thus weakening its impact.

If you are trying to optimize your blog title for social media, headlines should ideally stay between 8-14 words.

8. Follow a simple yet highly effective formula.

Numerical (or a powerful trigger word) + adjective + main/secondary keyword + solution/promise.

For instance, if you are writing about bathing puppies, you could say *18 Incredible Ways to Bathe a Puppy Outdoors*.

Think about writing a headline making a bold

promise applying this formula. For instance, to sell your old furniture in a day, the headline could be *How You Can Easily Sell Your Old Furniture in Less Than 24 Hours*. People really do not want to invest precious time reading something boring. They want action-packed and exciting content. These are the headlines that get your content read, and eventually, it will boost conversions.

Make reading the blog post worth people's time by creating headlines that not only grab their attention but also describe your post in an accurate, honest and enticing manner. Make it a proposition they cannot refuse, and an action they will not regret.

Here are some brilliant headline formulas

1. Do You Want To ------- Like Your Friends?

This is a classic social proof headline that tells the reader that many others are doing what is advertised or mentioned in the blog. It instills a fear of not wanting to be left behind. The reader should feel like they will miss something if they do not read the content or click on the link.

2. Here is One Neat Technique That is Really Helping People -----
3. Little Known Strategies For ------
4. Here's a Quick and Effective Way to -------
5. Warning! You May Be ------- (something unflattering)
6. 10 Proven Ways to (accomplishing a desired goal)
7. What You Should Know About ------ (something that impacts their life)
8. Are You Still Stuck with Eating Dairy? (Pose provocative questions that get your readers thinking).
9. 25 Hacks to (accomplishing the desired result). Easy yet effective, solution offering headline. It gets people looking for quick solutions hooked.
10. Now You Can Really Have ------------ (something desirable)
11. 15 Experts Share their Number One Child Nutrition Tip (the round-up headline

when you featuring experts/influencers in your niche to create a round-up for your blog)

12. How Eating Fruits and Vegetables Can Make You Fat (the unexpected pattern breaking headline. You can also use a reminder headline like Your Weight Doesn't Really Reveal Your Health.

Anything unexpected that challenges commonly accepted notions have a novelty factor attached to it, which makes people take notice. However, ensure that the headline is in sync with your content. If your headline says that eating vegetables can make you fat then mention in what way vegetables can make you fat. Do not create false headlines just to grab the reader's attention.

9. Use Topic generator sites and tools.

This one is a little known tip yet is my favorite for generating lots of cool blog post ideas and headlines.

Use a site like SEOPressor to come up with a bunch of search engine optimized (SEO) friendly and engaging headlines. You enter a keyword. Let's say acne, then go on to describe the keyword (is it is generic term or brand/product name, etc).

The results will return several attractive blog topics and headlines such as "5 Secrets About Acne Which Haven't Been Revealed in the Last 50 Years" or "You Will Never Believe These Bizarre Truths About Acne." HubSpot's blog topic generator is also worth using. Look at these sites for inspiration.

Chapter Three

Secrets for Curating and Rewriting Great Content

We know by know what a difference wow content and attention grabbing headlines can make when it comes to developing a seriously profitable blog. However, how do you constantly come up with power-packed content that interests and impact readers?

Fret not, I have your back there. I am spilling all the beans about digging out super powered content that has the potential to make your blog massively successful.

Content Curation

While content creation is about creating a piece of content (blog post, video, image or more) from scratch, curation is about gathering already existing content such as blog posts, social media updates or eBooks that are relevant to your niche, and sharing them with your readers/followers.

Several surveys have revealed that the number one challenge for blog owners or content marketers is to come up with sufficient quality content to build a more engaged social media audience and populate their blogs with top notch content.

Though it has its share of limitations, content curation has the following benefits:

- It helps build relationships with other bloggers and influencers. Content curation is like a brilliant synergy where everyone benefits from giving each other a larger audience. It helps build some amazing online partnerships with industry influencers.
  According to a Crowdtap study, 44% of industry experts work with other brands since it offers them a relevant opportunity for their audience, too.
- Content Curation saves time. If you are operating multiple blogs and social media channels, and do not have the time to

populate each of them with stellar content on a daily basis, content curation is like manna from heaven for your blog.

- Admit it. You cannot be a pro at everything. Content curation helps you fill the gaps that you may have left as a creator. Sourcing content from diverse, reputable channels gives you the advantage of bringing more variety to your content.

Having said that, ensure that if you use content from other sources, link attribution is given to the writer and blog page. Seek proper permissions before using someone else's content. Ensure that the terms are clear before posting, so there's no confusion or legal hassles later.

Have you heard about Upworthy? Yes, the same viral site that posts interesting content with catchy, clickbait style headlines.

When they launched, they became a roaring success only by repackaging and curating a majority of their content from other sources and posting it using sexy and shocking headlines. They eventually transitioned into content creation, but a lot of the early success was their ability to repackage promising content from varied sources and presenting it in a more stunning, attention-grabbing style.

4 Ways for Finding Great Content in Your Niche

1. Go to a BuzzSumo. Enter your topic or domain in the search option, and click go. You will be presented with the most popular content related to your topic, including statistics such as numbers of social media shares and pages that link back to it.

2. Google Trends is another great place for digging out great content based on organic searches. So, if you want to have a nice combination of content that is popular on both social media and search engines,

include Google Trends into your content curation strategy. You will see an entire list of trending stories for the last 24 hours. Enter a specific topic if you want to gauge the changing popularity of a topic and the interest it generates among readers of varied geographic regions.

3. A lot of viral sites pick up their content from aggregators such as Reddit. It is indeed the "Front Page of the Internet" as it describes itself. There's a goldmine of hidden content in subreddits on virtually any topic under the sun.

   Unlike other content aggregation channels, Reddit's content is ranked by freshness and popularity score, which makes it an ideal platform for digging out trending content, especially about lesser known niches.

   On signing up, a user automatically has

access to a a large amount of content. You have to manually unsubscribe from subreddits that aren't of any interest to you. There's plenty of opportunity to get your hands on little known, detailed, multiperspective and information-rich content.

4. Use the power of question and answer sites. Quora is another great place for finding informative and detailed content presented as answers to a query by most experts in their fields. So you may have skin experts offering the best home remedies for black heads or a practicing Stoic sharing his insightful beliefs about the philosophy of Stoicism.

There are other question and answer sites such as Wiki Answers, How Stuff Works and Yahoo Answers, where you can unearth a lot of interesting stuff related to your niche.

5 Stellar Tips Used by Professionals for Rewriting Existing Content

Rewriting has gained a sort of notoriety on the online content world owing to the misconceptions people hold about it. It is not simply altering a few words or inserting a few synonymous to make it appear original.

Rewriting content is about repackaging existing content to lend it a fresh appeal, while still retaining the essence of the original.

If you already have a large bank of blog posts or original content, it is easy to repurpose it into newer and fresher pieces of content instead of starting from scratch and hitting a roadblock. Cut your time by using these valuable strategies for repurposing existing pieces into stellar content.

1. Transform lists into standalone content pieces. If you have several list-based posts such as "7 crackling smart investment options" and other similar posts, you can very well convert it into individual blog

posts. Each investment option can be turned into a separate blog post by listing its features, merits, and demerits. Fleshing out each point also gives your readers more detailed and insightful information.

It gives you an opportunity to build on or expand existing ideas by conducting research. Repacking lists into individual articles also establishes your expertise in a specific subject. Add a few case studies or examples to make the posts more comprehensive and interesting to read.

2. Combine multiple posts into a summary post. You may have written multiple blog posts about child psychology or about improving learning and development among children. Use key point from each blog to create a summary blog post like "Top Tips for Improving Your Child's Learning Abilities" or "5 Important Things Parents Must Know About Development

Learning." It is actually just the opposite of the first tip.

3. Revamp old posts for a brand new audience. You may have written something keeping in mind a specific audience. For instance, operational challenges faced by nonprofit organizations. You may want to cater to another type of audience; for instance, small business owners. While the general framework will remain similar, you will have to tweak a few points to suit profit organizations. This will help you target different sets of audience in a more focused manner with almost similar content.

4. Update existing posts with latest information. In today's fast paced world, things change at the blink of an eyelid. There are forever new developments and updates, especially in the world of internet

marketing and technology. The blog post you drafted a couple of years ago may be relevant, but there may be newer trends and developments that you readers may want to know.

For instance, if you wrote a post about best SEO practices for bloggers in 2015, you may want to update it by including newer SEO dynamics and trends that held relevance over the past year. Make it a practice to review old blog posts periodically to gauge if they can be updated with fresh statistics, newer examples/case studies or important recent developments. Google and other search engines love fresh, updated and time-relevant content.

5. Focus on ideas, not words. Even the most seasoned writers and bloggers fall into the trap of copying words above ideas. Do not restructure the content sentence by

sentence or even paragraph by paragraph just because you are rewriting an existing piece of content. Instead of focusing on expressions and composition of the original writer, try and concentrate on ideas. Rewriting is not about shuffling a few words and sentences. The objective is to understand what exactly is being conveyed, and then communicate it in your own, distinct style.

6. Add fresh, new ideas. Yes, we can all have our Eureka moments while writing, where we think of something fresh and exciting that hasn't been covered by the original writer or our original post. Utilize this moment of epiphany to the fullest, and include these new insights into your post. You may want to include an interesting piece of research or share an example or add your own unique perspective on the matter.

No rule says one cannot include a fresh element to rewritten content. Do not be afraid to reinvent and improve the post with newer insights. It will only help in making the article appear fresher and more distinct from the original.

7. Re-writing headlines. Alerting the headline to give your post a new angle is the easiest way to begin the rewriting process. Find something that is still relevant to your post but lends it a slightly diverse perspective or angle. You may also want to include a different keyword or optimize the post for Google or social media channels.

8. Make the introductory paragraph unique. The opening paragraph is your chance to grab the interest of your competitor or send them running to competitors. Make it an enticing proposition by including something of value that does not feature in

the original article. It can be anything from a statistic to a new piece of research to an attention-grabbing pro tip. Give readers a strong reason to read further even if they have read the original post. Avoid fluff in the opening paragraph (or anywhere in the post).

Another neat tip is to reinvent the layout of your post by including different headings and subheadings. You may want to expand the article by breaking it into sub headings if there aren't any in the original. It will also make your piece more scan-able and readable.

Finding Jaw Dropping Beautiful Images

Images are an important component of your blog profit strategy. They complement your written words to create a more wholesome experience for the reader. All top blogs use attention grabbing images to communicate their message compellingly. Using the right images also boost your search engine optimization efforts.

So how to do you find images that make your blog posts look amazing? Here are some expert tips to find the perfect images for your post.

Take Pictures Yourself

This really saves you the trouble of finding the perfect and most relevant images for your blog. There are no hassles about seeking permissions, paying for high-quality stock photos or digging into the creative commons public domain.

If you are writing a post and have a fair idea about how to represent it best visually, use you a camera or your smartphone to take high-quality pictures. Ensure they are well-lit to make them appear high-resolution images. Go outdoors and take pictures in bright light to make them look more flattering.

Paid Royalty-Free Stock Images

If you have a higher budget, you can buy royalty free images from iStockPhoto or Shutterstock. They have a huge assortment of images for virtually any conceivable topic under the sun.

Bloggers/publishers have the option of paying a one-time fee for using an image several times for various purposes (without any fixed time limit for using it) or sign up for a monthly/yearly subscription that allows you to download a fixed number of images per month/year.

These photographs are high vector images that make your site look professional, and save you from getting into any copyright trouble later.

Free Photo Resources

There are many sites such as Pixabay, Pexels, Unsplash and more where you can get access to a whole bunch of high-quality and on-topic images. Simply enter a few keywords related to the picture in the search option and pick the ones that fit well with your post. Pixabay has a fairly good collection of images, which can be used even for commercial purposes without attribution.

Just ensure that you do not use the sponsored images that show at the top of your search since these are the pay to use images. It is fairly easy to tell because the sponsored images have a distinct watermark.

Ensure you read the terms of every picture you are using very carefully to avoid getting into copyright issues trouble. Some pictures may require an attribution (credit to the owner), some may not.

Even though the prospect of using free images seems lucrative, things change pretty rapidly in the online business world. You never know when the original owner of the image may change its terms of use.

You may not have a large budget in the initial stages of your blog, which makes these free resources a good place, to begin with. Once you start raking in some profits, it is a good idea to invest in royalty-free paid stock images.

Others Blogs and Pages

You cannot simply get images from other people's blogs and pages by performing a simple Google image search. It could lead to serious copyright violations and legal trouble.

If you really like a particular image that's on another blog, begin by complimenting the owner/photo and seek their permission clearly for using the photo. Always seek permission before posting the image and proceed only when you have documented permission stating their consent for using their original work on your blog.

Give them proper credit by mentioning them as the source and linking back to their page or website below the image.

Creative Commons License (CC)

Images under the Creative Commons license are in public domain, which means you are free to use, reuse and distribute them. Depending on individual Creative Commons (CC) licenses, users can use images for commercial purposes or create derivatives of the image.

There are several CC licenses, which means you have to carefully go through the license of each image to know what is permissible under the specific license. To be on the safer side, always attribute all images under the Creative Commons license to their rightful owner.

Wikimedia Commons and Flickr are some great sources for finding CC licensed images. Again while using images from these sources check all licenses by clicking on the individual terms of use/some rights reserved link. You will learn the terms of use of that particular photo such as, whether it can be shared, adapted and used commercially. Also, it will be mentioned if an attribution link to the owner of the image is required.

Here's a quick breakdown of various Creative Commons Licenses

Attribution: This means that the user is required to attribute the image to its original owner in the specified manner. You also have to be mindful of the fact that the image should not be used in a manner which implies that the owner of the image endorses your page/brand or you in any way.

Share-Alike: This clause means the image should not be held under different or restrictive terms than those laid down by the original creator.

Non Commercial: The image should only be utilized for non-commercial purposes.

No Derivative Works: The image is to be used only as it is without altering it or creating derivatives of it.

9 Kick-Ass Resources to Enhance Your Content Writing from Good to Wow

Of course, you have great content and the best formats to present it. However, the tools listed below can expedite the process or make it even more effective. Here are five resources that should be in the tool box of every content creator or marketer.

1. Grammarly

This is really your must have tool when it comes to writing grammatically correct and smooth flowing blogs. The software helps scan your text for any grammatical, punctuation and spelling errors really fast, thus making it appear professional. As a resource, it gives more direction and clarity to your writing. It helps optimize your post and makes it easier to read.

2. Hemingway

Hemingway is a virtual editing tool that is hugely popular among content writers, with good reason. It is a user-friendly text editing software, which highlights complex sentences and offers suggestions for eliminating unwanted adverbs. It also converts drab reading passive sentences into a more actionable active voice.

There is a tracker, which shows you the final count of words, characters, and paragraphs. You can fine-tune the text structure to make it more appealing and readable. Once you are finish making changes, the file can be exported in an .html format.

3. Ideaflip

As a content creator, learn to develop ideas rather than working on the first one that strikes you. Brainstorming is integral to the process of creating wow-worthy content, and Ideaflip helps you do that.

Instead of writing everything on a piece of paper, use Ideaflip. It offers a highly visual, dynamic and interactive platform for developing ideas.

4. Power Thesaurus

Power Thesaurus is a crowdsourced app that does not have any ads (yay!). It is a hit with writers for its elegant interface and streamlined search options. The app is always updated with the newest linguistic trends, which makes it a must-have ammo in your writer warfare kit.

5. Ahrefs

Ahrefs is several SEO resources that can push your blog content into the next league by ranking higher on search engines. Some tools help you keep a close eye on your competitors' SEO tactics and enhance your own content.

6. Canva

We have discussed the power of using compelling visuals in drawing people to your blog. Canva helps you accomplish that goal, with its aesthetically pleasant layouts and high utility value. Use it when you want to add some sparkle to your visual content. It allows graphically challenged folks to create professional and stunning looking visual presentations, infographics and social media cover images. They have a wide assortment of templates that can be adapted for any niche.

7. StackEdit

StackEdit is a handy tool for converting text files into .html or exporting them from Google Docs or Word without altering the formatting. It is an inbuilt browser mark-down that has a ton of great features such as shortcuts that make your writing more unique, has a variety of themes and several layouts. Also, the spell checker is compatible with several languages. The best part? StackEdit can be synced with a variety of tools such as WordPress and Dropbox. It is also available for offline use.

9. Yoast WordPress Plugin

Even though you do not have to stuff your posts with a bunch of keywords, you still have to make your posts more searchable for readers. What's the point of writing phenomenal blog posts when your readers are not able to find them?

Yoast lets you know how optimized your content is regarding a specific keyword and content analysis. It offers tons of helpful suggestions about how to optimize your post to please search engines and readers. It also includes a handy site map feature, which boosts your search engine page indexing efforts.

Content Scheduling

A well-organized and comprehensive content schedule allows you to stay on track with your editorial goals. It helps you save time, and take on multiple tasks, while still running your blog on auto-pilot. Here are some power-packed content scheduling tips.

1. Have a clear brand/blog persona and start by brainstorming content that matches your persona. The content should address your target audience's most pressing issues. Aspire to be a trusted and respected source of information related to the industry.

2. Plenty of marketers test their content on social media before creating full-fledged

blog posts about the same. The experimental post can be thought-provoking, fresh, engaging, humorous and exclusive. Gauge if your content has the potential to be popular on social media.

3. Create a content calendar for 1 to 3 months in advance, and keep adding to it. Bigger events such as Q&A's, interviews, eBooks, product releases, conferences, podcasts, live videos can be announced once a date is locked.

4. Social media posts are best scheduled in advance unless you want to post about recent developments.

5. As a good practice, create 3-4 long blog posts a week, a couple of SlideShare presentations, syndication on sites such Tumblr, 4-5 daily comments from influencers around the web, an infographic every two weeks and a monthly eBook.

6. Google Calendar is a great resource for planning and scheduling content.
7. Keep a close eye on trends too. You may be the most fastidious planner, but you can never completely rely on scheduled content. Keep a close eye on latest trends for cashing in on latest stories. Monitor your content analytics closely. Your content calendar will keep evolving according to your readers' response.

If it is not working for you, try different types of content. Look around at what competitors are doing in a dynamic and ever-changing world of content marketing.

How to Schedule Posts on WordPress

For publishing posts to your audience's time zone, go to the WordPress dashboard and head to settings. Tap on the General Menu option. Select the appropriate time zone and click "Save Changes."

There is a "Publish meta box" on the right-hand corner of the "Edit" option adjacent to the Publish button. Set the date and time the date you wish to publish your post.

Schedule you blog post at the given date and time. Tap on the "Schedule" button.

For rescheduling posts, select "Edit" adjacent to the right-hand side of the Schedule tab. Set the new date and time for publishing the post and update it.

The same process can be used for re-publishing posts that were previously published at a given date and time. You can also create a new post and make it appear as if it was published earlier by following the same process. There are lots WordPress plugins for scheduling posts, too.

Chapter Four: 14 Types of Content That Can Sky-Rocket Your Blog Traffic

There's no short cut to success. If you want to build a profitable blog, you have got to put in a lot of stellar content out there for your audience. Not just that, you have to diversify your content strategy to use different types of content formats that work. There are plenty of fresh and interesting ways to present your content and grow the blog. Don't know how?

Here's a list of different types of content that are proven to draw a large audience, increase engagement, boost SEO and help you build a solid brand.

1. How-to Posts

Everyone loves step-by-step how-to tutorials which make the process of learning something new or solving a problem fairly simple. Any solution showing a how-to post or video is a golden opportunity for attracting a targeted audience. If laid out in an easy-to-understand, step-by-step and detailed manner, these posts/videos perform extremely well and go viral really quick.

Pro Tip: Make it a long and detailed post, almost like a short report or book. It is great if you can include images or screenshots describing each step.

2. Latest News

You will not believe the number of pages that make money on the internet purely on shock value. Of course, unless your blog is an all-news blog, you can also use breaking news related to your industry in combination with other pieces of information.

The biggest advantage of breaking and latest news is that you do not have to create it from scratch. You just have to put together the most important bits of information and rewrite it. Lots of blog owners curate news pieces from other sources and link back to them.

People love to follow interesting or important pieces of information related to their industry or area of interest. It goes a long way in establishing your blog's credibility and authority, which is important if you want to get people to buy from you.

The way to get it right is by opting for quality over quantity. Do not populate your viral fed or blog with too many click-bait style breaking news pieces. Position yourself as an idea influencer in your industry. Offer only high value, useful and insightful content. You can either publish a piece of breaking news daily or create weekly/monthly news updates.

3. Infographics

Infographics are hugely popular, especially when it comes to social sharing. People love to share content that is presented in a comprehensive, yet condensed, format.

Human beings are wired to be attracted to anything that's presented in an easy-to-understand, visual format. We dig interactivity, research, and stats that are packaged in a more digestible form.

Creating appealing and share-worthy infographics is time-consuming. You can do it yourself using an app like Canva or Photoshop if you are more graphically inclined or you can hire someone from elance, Guru or oDesk to do it for you. Visual.ly is also a good place for getting started with infographics.

If you do not want to make your infographics from scratch, share existing ones. There are lots of handy infographics available to be embedded through a simple Google search. Just ensure you have the permission to use it, and credit it to the right source.

4. Lists

Again, it is no secret that people love lists, which explains the barrage of "10 best things to do" and

"30 best places to head to" etc. on your social feed. Readers love content that is presented to them in a systematic, digestible and structured manner.

Can you really resist clicking on list-based headlines that sound interesting and informative? This is the classic go to post for any content creator or marketer.

There's a neat little trick to get these posts right. Start by introducing a problem. List possible solutions for the problem, and offer a strong, actionable conclusion that nudges the reader to act upon these solutions.

Provide value to the reader by making these list posts as detailed and comprehensive as possible. Most Important – be sure to give these posts attention-grabbing and nonmisleading headlines. Your "10 Good Content Formats" (even if exceptionally well-written) may not grab as many views as "10 Outrageously Successful Content Formats That You Aren't Using Yet." If you need people to be all ears to your message, convey it with a punch.

Pro Tip: do not just list all the points to read like a grocery list. Take the time to discuss each point, offer your own insights, present numbers and justify the item's inclusion in the list. For instance, if you are telling people Greece is one of the best places for destination weddings in 2017, tell them why too (number of tourist, great weather, visitor friendly conditions, easy laws, etc.). Always focus on offering a strong value proposition to your audience.

5. Round-Ups

Expert round-ups may seem easy because you are not creating the content yourself. However, it may take time and effort to put it all together.

Round-ups are nothing but posts where several experts in your subject share their number one tip or answer a focused question related to topic. For instance, if you are running a blog in the internet marketing domain, you may pose questions such as "What is your number one tip for growing social media followers or generating traffic for your blog?"

Round ups work because they are beneficial for everyone involved. Your readers get access to a whole list of expert tips. The influencers get to reinforce their expert status by sharing your post among their followers and readers. You get plenty of shares from different experts (imagine 20 different experts all sharing your posts among their followers to demonstrate that they have been featured as experts yet again).

However, it is not easy to put together a round-up. You need to approach influencers and get them to agree to be featured in the round-up. However, if you can pull off a few fantastic round-ups, you may manage to draw a swarm of blog traffic.

Some good tools for finding influencers in your niche are BuzzSumo, Traackr, Linkdex and more. You can also search on social media using popular hashtags or keywords related to your niche.

6. PowerPoint Presentations and Slides

This is a highly proven format that seldom goes wrong. It makes for a visual and interactive way to get across information to a focused audience. Slideshare is a great platform for sharing information in a slide show format.

Keep it a mix of information and entertainment. Do not make the readers feel like they are being held hostage in a boring meeting or the boardroom. Even the most serious topic can do with a dash of humor. This is a simple yet highly effective way to put across a ton of information in a quick, understandable format.

7. Case Studies

Case studies are a perfect way to flaunt your expertise in the industry. The ideal way is to take up something that you have worked on yourself. If you can present to your readers how a particular approach helped others meet their goals, etc., you will automatically appear more authoritative and credible to them. If you are selling a product or service on your blog, it is a good idea to include a case study about the value it offered someone. You are doing nothing but validating your product or reinforcing its merit.

A great case study is similar to a how to post, only more focused, insightful and detailed. Sum it up with the lessons readers can take back from it along with a powerful conclusion that gets them thinking. End with a strong call to action.

Pro tip: Do not simply rattle away facts and figures to appear intelligent. Weave the fact and figures into a story to make the case study more relatable and identifiable. Adding a human touch to it makes it more engaging than a clinical approach of merely rattling off facts.

8. Reviews

These are your manna from heaven where blog profits are concerned. Review-based posts are great for affiliate marketers promoting the products and services of others.

Richly written, pictorial and detailed reviews, which are presented in an easy to follow format are hugely lucrative.

Ensure the reviews are broken up into short paragraphs. Include lots of bullet points (pros and cons of a product or service), tables and visuals. Tables can be used to demonstrate what the product or service offers in comparison to similar products or services.

The ideal structure is beginning with an introduction, sharing your experience with the product (merits and demerits), and a conclusion (stating whether you would recommend the product to your readers). Summarize the key points of the review to facilitate quick reading for those who do not have much time at their disposal.

Finally, include a powerful call to action.

9. Guides, eBooks or Short Reports

If you think there is a huge need for detailed and lengthy information related to a particular area of your niche, go ahead and create a detailed guide or short report for it. These are more extensive in content and visuals than blog posts. You can offer your readers to download it in PDF format. What's more?

This can be a huge bait for getting interested readers to sign up for your email list. Enlist the assistance of a graphic designer to help you put together the layout and cover for the guide or report.

If you want to make the value proposition even more, create an entire eBook related to the topic. You will get ideas for the book simply by keeping your ears close to what your readers are saying. For instance, if you own a travel blog and keep posting about your global adventures, readers may ask you about how you manage to travel to so many destinations or your favorite tips for traveling cheap. This is a great opportunity to dive head on into creating an eBook about budget travel tips. You get the drift? Identify an area where people are desperately looking for information within your niche. It does not have to be a 200 page document. You can create a short eBooks with an eye-catching cover and gripping, valuable content. This is also an effective way to attract more readers, social media followers and subscribers.

10. Memes

Admit it, we have all shared memes that have made us laugh or touched us deeply. Memes are not just great for social sharing but also help your readers take a breather from more long-winded and serious content, and look at the lighter side of a situation.

Memes can be made without much time or effort using resources such as Meme Generator or Quick Meme. They can be customized for any subject or industry. If you want to put your point across in a smarter and more light hearted way, memes are the way to go.

Of course, they cannot be standalone pieces of content on your blog. However, they can be used for gaining some social media traction or complementing text posts.

To avoid any miscommunication or controversy, ensure that you do a little background research to understand the connotations attached to different characters and what they stand for. Do not blindly lift images to create memes without understanding the attached significance. The last thing you want is a backfired effort.

11. Interviews

Interviews are another great way to impress your audience. The more authoritative and influential your interviewee, the better it is for your blog credibility. Your followers/readers can learn a lot when it comes straight from the horse's mouth. Pick an important figure within your industry, and get them to feature for a full-length interview on your blog.

You can either do a video interview, a live podcast or send a list of questions for the person to answer in a textual format. Look at Mixergy for instance. The site is dedicated to interviewing accomplished people.

How do you go about conducting an interview?

Begin by introducing the expert. Highlight their accomplishments to make the prospect of listening to them attractive for readers.

Prepare a list of questions in advance by doing some background research about the experts. Of course, follow up questions will pop up throughout the interview. However, a set of prepared questions will lend it a structure. Conclude the interview by doing a quick summary of all the interesting and important things discussed in the interview. Offer your audience/readers a clear takeaway. Make a conclusion more urgent and actionable.

12. Printable Check Lists and To-Do Lists

This one sure makes the life of your readers easier by compiling all the scattered tasks or items into a single, organized list. It ensures that a task is done more efficiently, and nothing is left out. Wedding checklists, travel checklists, new baby checklists, blog creation checklist, etc., are extremely popular among their target audience.

Give your readers the option of saving these checklists in a printable PDF format. Checklists are great when it comes to getting readers to sign up for your mailing list.

13. Videos

Videos are a brilliant way to make your content both appealing and informative to your readers. Multiple studies have pointed to the fact that people register things more powerfully when they see it being done than simply reading about it.

Visuals strike a chord with your target audience and add variety to your content strategy. Social is becoming increasingly visual in nature. It is all about eye-catching visuals and slickly packaged, easy-to-follow videos. Also, YouTube is the world's second most widely used search engine, which gives you a fair idea about the amount of video content people are consuming.

Make videos that show off your blog's/brand's personality. It does not cost a lot to make basic, good quality videos. Use a smart phone for capturing a video, along with an editing software tool such as Camtasia.

Experiment with multiple video formats like screencasts (talking into the camera), fast paced videos or explainer videos. Keep it short, power-packed and to the point, since people do not really have the time to view videos that ramble endlessly. Plus, putting up your video on YouTube boosts your social signal with Google, who sees all the engagement as a validation of your content and popularity among readers.

Pro Tip: Give your videos a more well-rounded

context by including a blog post or a video transcript (that viewers can later refer).

14. Spotlight Posts

People love human interest stories that relate to other people. When you create personal spotlight posts, you instantly engage followers emotionally. It makes the content more interesting and digestible for people. For instance, you can create a behind the scenes story featuring your employees or clients.

Make your blog more personal by showing your audience how it works. It will invariably make your brand appear more human, identifiable and approachable.

Alternatively, you can take advantage of a personal spotlight post by interviewing someone in or out of your company. This is especially beneficial if you can wrangle someone with a recognizable name, but this is not a necessity.

Personal spotlight posts can be beneficial in

making you seem more personal, but they should not constitute the majority of your campaign. Use them as a complementary element of your strategy, serving as an occasional alternative-style post. Also be sure to rotate the subject of your post, or else your readers could get bored.

Chapter Five: 10 Content Marketing Tips to Take Your Blog into the Next League

Now that we know why content creation is so integral to the process of creating profitable blogs and how to create stellar content, let's look at how you can widen your reach and draw an even bigger audience to your blog by using these highly actionable content marketing strategies.

1. Guest Blogging

One of the easiest and most effective ways to spread the word about your blog and come off as more authoritative at the same time is to write guest blog posts. You find similar blogs in your niche or popular industry websites and create insightful posts for them.

Make it well-researched, detailed and analytical to position yourself as an expert on the subject. You will not just end up building brand authority but also draw a swarm of traffic to your blog.

Include a link to your blog in the author bio along with a power-packed description.

2. Social Media Ads

Social ads are a good way to gain some traction for your posts. You do not need to throw away hundreds of dollars on promoting your blog. Even a post boost of $15-20 can help you gain decent exposure if you have put out amazingly share-worthy content. Ads (especially Facebook ads) give you a very large yet focused audience.

3. Do not Be Overtly Promotional

Do not be overtly promotional when it comes to content marketing. Remember the purpose is to take your reader/potential buyer through a buying cycle. Do not go full throttle, jet boating on your customers immediately. Let them gain some value before you start seeking conversions.

4. Start with a Framework

You may not always have products or services to talk about, especially in the earlier stages of the blog. Skip the product/service talk and focus on a larger framework (that impacts readers) that deals with themes, ideas and issues. Keep the topics closely connected and relevant to your target audience.

5. Do not Monetize Until You Rank

Garnering links to your posts can be really tough. Make it simpler by not combining your content marketing (drawing an audience to your blog) with monetizing efforts. Do not undertake any money making activity until you rank well. Once you have undertaken sufficient outreach activities, rank well, and draw a decent audience of regular readers, only then start your monetization methods. Do not ruin your blog's long term chances by trying to make a few quick bucks from your blog early on.

Of course, you may not have the luxury to wait until you make money. People need quick returns to meet their expenses. If you can afford to hold off earning from your blog (until you rank well for competitive keywords and draw a decent traffic), you can gain a lot more in the long run.

6. Leverage Email Campaigns

Much as new-age internet marketers would have you believe otherwise, email campaigns are far from dead. Emails continue to play a vital role in the process of generating traffic for your blog.

Send interesting, informative and content rich newsletters to your email subscribers. Integrate content into a logical sales funnel that compels your target audience to buy. For instance, if you are selling some products related to baby nutrition, try to offer some tips or recipes related to nutrition.

Establish your expertise in the field of child nutrition, and get readers to trust you by populating their email feed with valuable and useful content.

7. Connect with Influencers

Create a list of influencers within your industry

using a tool like Little Bird. Use social media to connect with them. Cross promote each other's blogs. Retweet the content of popular influencers for them to notice you and follow your blog, and eventually share your content among their followers.

Get them to write guest posts for you and share links to the post on their social media pages. This way their hundreds of followers will find you and start following you too.

8. Create Evergreen Content

Evergreen content are pieces that stay relevant irrespective of its time of publication. You can create tons of free how-to guides and small reports that remain relevant to your audience, which saves you the hassle of updating the content periodically.

9. Use Your Best Headlines for Pay Per Click Ads

If you are using PPC campaigns to promote your

blog, repurpose your best-performing headlines into an attention-grabbing ad copy. If you realized that a headline worked particularly well with your target audience, repurpose into your ad copy. There really isn't much difference between blog post content and PPC ads regarding the angles that are used to hook readers/customers (such as emotionally tugging angles, strong action verbs, and clear benefits). If you are not sure between different set of headlines, run A/B test to gauge how each headline is performing individually. You will know what types of headlines or content ad copy resonates best with your audience.

10. Keep it Consistent with Your Brand Voice

Content marketing is the best way to develop, refine and reinforce your brand/blog's voice. However, even the biggest brands fail to identify their voice or clearly define it.

Ensure that your content reflects the consistency

and continuity of your brand. Review your editorial stands periodically to ascertain that the tone and voice of your brand are consistent with the blog persona in general. Are you positioning yourself as a fun, youthful, fresh blog for a younger audience? Are you positioning yourself as an authoritative and serious source of information in your industry?

While drafting or marketing each post, ask how the content can advance you blog's persona, goals or value? What does the tone of your blog reflect? Does it reinforce your company's values?

11. Answer Complex Questions Using Long Tail Keywords

Attempt to answer complicated questions related to your niche with more targeted and specific, long-tail keywords. You will increase your chances of ranking for a larger number of more focused keywords, where customers are actively seeking information.

While some content creators and marketers

believe in writing naturally without adopting a keyword based approach, others strongly advocate targeting your audience with long tail or more focused keywords. Before creating content that you are using for boosting your content marketing efforts, make a comprehensive list of the keywords you are looking to rank for.

By doing a quick scan or survey of some popular forums within your industry, you will know exactly what your readers are looking for. Make dedicated and detailed posts for addressing these queries, and post them of these forums (if permitted). You can also leave lots of smart tips or ideas or little-known information on these forum threads and include a link to your blog in the author bio.

Conclusion

Thank you for downloading my eBook *Blog Writing: The content creation blueprint (how to master content creation to propel your blog on to the next level and make even more serious money online)*.

I sincerely hope the book was able to help you gain insights into the process of content creation for running a highly profitable blog.

The next step is to stop planning and start taking action. There are tons of little-known tips, tried and tested strategies and actionable wisdom nuggets for helping blog publishers build their blog content, increase their authority and establish an equation of trust with potential buyers. From beginners to seasoned blog publishers and marketers, everyone can benefit from the easy-to-follow yet insanely effective strategies discussed in this book.

Finally, if you enjoyed reading the book, please take some time out to share your thoughts by posting a review on Amazon. It would be highly appreciated.

Here's to being a highly successful blog publisher!

www.ingramcontent.com/pod-product-compliance
Lightning Source LLC
Chambersburg PA
CBHW030443220526
45464CB00006B/2403